Paradise Resc

Let's Get Visual

The Power of Envisioning Success in Business and Life

David Stannard

Dedication

You have given us our Mission,
filled our (picture)Vision and
fuelled our Passion.
Thank you Cardan, Bordeaux
and everyone who has connected
with project Paradise Rescued
across the world.

Failure is not an option.

ISBN: 978-0-6485962-0-2

Published by David Stannard, VIC 3113, Australia
www.paradiserescued.com

Contents

Foreword

From the first day of business at Paradise Rescued I have been passionate about the use of social media, and the use of pictures in particular. Strangely to me, this wasn't a commonly shared idea in the wine business; almost no one else seemed to use pictures in the same way; would this be my advantage? The idea of taking pictures of beautiful wine, vineyards, wineries, and happy people together with a strong brand-image just seemed natural and compelling to me.

To help build our new brand and marketing strategy, I joined an on line monthly webinar group called the 'Social Media Professionals'. We met once a year for a two-day face-to-face meeting and intense boot camp style workshop, collaborating as a team. At one boot camp in particular, I remember being asked to present on how and why I used visual images. Until this point I hadn't really given that the question much thought. "It just felt natural to me." With the step-change in digital technology allowing phones to take pictures and share them around the world through different social media, picture media was now possible. With my 'big business' manufacturing hard-hat on, I had also witnessed first-hand the successful impact that the visual management of data and performance could achieve.

As I prepared the presentation, I was challenged to try and understand why my approach of using original visual material was working. What was so special about a picture rather than a paragraph of text? I rushed off to the Internet followed quickly by a review of all my leadership literature.

The answers weren't there. What was I going to present now? I had to propose my own thesis!

I made a gut-feel guess that I was a very "visual" person, whatever that might be, and I wrote my presentation around that concept, comparing it to our other human senses. I let the boot camp group agree or disagree with my proposed theory as they wished.

The 'visual' theme seemed to strike a common chord with the small audience around the table. I could see the lights come on in their minds and the start of a visual social-media conversion process start.

Yet, I needed to follow through as to why 'visual' was so powerful in relation to our other senses and why simple pictures had such leadership potential and power. I needed to understand at a psychological level why my gut-instinct might be true. The (picture)Vision process was beginning to take shape.

In this book, I will take you on a journey to a place where you too can harness that potential 'visual' power for your personal, business, or organisational future; helping to create more positive and sustainable results at all levels.

Let's get started on that journey. Let's get visual.

David Stannard

Part A

Vision
Mission
Passion

1

The Trifecta

Why visions, missions, and passions are all important

Harvest Day is like no other at Paradise Rescued in Cardan, Bordeaux. It is the culmination of one or more seasons of work in the vineyard, during which we never forget that pruning and overall care of a vineyard in a particular season can have a significant effect several years in the future. It is also a time of local celebration for the niche sustainability strategy that has maintained the heritage of a rural community. Local villagers, customers, team-members, contractors, shareholders and stakeholders from all corners of the globe come together to pick the grapes and set in motion an exciting new vintage of award winning, organic Bordeaux-wine.

No matter what the early autumn weather presents, the team is in good spirits, energised by hot coffee served with fresh croissants or choclatines. Our international team goes to work with dedication, precision and laughter as the sun comes up. Their goal is a common one: to cut, pick, and separate the best, and healthiest fruit from the vineyard and deliver it to the winery undamaged, where it will be de-stemmed, and gently crushed before it's loaded into the stainless steel vats, ready to start the making of a new wine. The higher the quality of the fruit, harvest and wine, the better the celebration for all concerned.

Revisiting Cardan

It sounds like a fairy tale of collaboration, the kind of thing one wants to read about all businesses, teams and organisations, but we rarely do. No one factor alone can create this alignment.

"Hey, David, when is the *patron* going to start work today?" comes the cry in French from one of our neighbours and good friends. My role on harvest day as patron (or boss/owner) is mixed, varied and most definitely without a job description. It is the team's strong preference, mine too, that I am there on site at the property. Other circumstances have sometimes prevented this from happening, but it is clearly where I should, and want to, be as the leader. The question is shouted in jest and enjoyed by all as the laughter echoes across the Cabernet Franc vineyard. My role on the day is chief media officer, film producer, logistics/communications manager, occasional decision maker and general team-spare wherever required.

I'm also expected to cut a few bunches of grapes ceremoniously before passing round the traditional 'Swiss' glass of white wine to toast the health of the vintage; which also enables me to thank everyone for their effort and support on the day and throughout the season. As I meet with harvesters, both new and returning, I am able to explain how and why the Paradise Rescued project started. Standing in any part of the vineyard it is easy to see the 12th century village on the small hill to the west and our friends' village-houses up the slope to the east. I explain that the reason for the project is to maintain a green buffer between the two which sustains the rural culture and nature of the village. A brief history of how it all came about is usually received with a lot of understanding nodding heads and enthusiastic support, but everyone begins to understand that every day and every year that Paradise Rescued succeeds is a 'win/win' for the community. The **Mission** is crystal clear.

Back up at the house and property, also known as Paradise Rescued HQ, there is a hive of activity in and around the entrance to the winery. Whenever I talk with friends about 'owning' a winery, their imagination rapidly conjures up a mental picture of a large building neatly filled with rows of vats and a room full of barrels, which is simply not the case. Our start-up plan was to have a small-function winery. Don't get me wrong, making outstanding red wine requires a lot of skill but the equipment required to make it all happen is remarkably simple and cost effective. Small stainless-steel vats – our so called 'microcuves' – together with a few oak barrels are a powerful duo supplemented by several smaller hand-tools for different winemaking operations.

Outside the winery doors leading away from the Paradise Rescued property and to our westerly neighbour's old farmhouse, is the new Merlot vineyard. This vineyard comprises the small, now 61-year-old block of vines that we recovered from their near-death experience in 2011 with patient and loving recovery by Pascale, our vigneronne. Higher up the slope, bordering the winery is the new Merlot parcel of vines, that one can call babies no longer, as they have made such an impressive and vigorous start to their careers, already producing small, restricted quantities of high-quality certified organic fruit. Their impressive health is in stark contrast to other third-party vineyards around them who receive a different kind of love and viticultural model. Back in 2011, this land was a broken-down mess of old Sémillon vines that had fallen into serious disrepair.

This so-called Phoenix project is a testament to the business model, tactical planning and clear **Vision** that preceded its implementation.

As the harvest team finishes their work, they happily return carrying the last grapes in their 'cagette' baskets up to the winery. Vigneronne Pascale, is the last to return having carried out one final inspection of the Cabernet Franc vineyard. As she returns to the property, she allows herself a quick stop for a drink and a chat before convening a quick leadership team-meeting with myself and Albane, her daughter and team Paradise Rescued winemaker plus organic viticultural advisor. Together, we review the fruit just picked before agreeing on the strategy for vinification, then Pascale goes to work again, checking every detail twice over and then finally sits down to the harvest meal that the catering team has prepared in the kitchen.

Pascale organises the whole day from the first croissant to the last scoop of ice cream, and everything in between. When visitors and media come to the winery they always remark on Pascale's energy, attention to detail and love for what she does. "She looks after her vines as if they were her children" is a popular observation.

Pascale doesn't have a job; she has an incredible **Passion**.

Why all three are important

In my first book *From Cabbage Patch to Cabernet Franc*, I introduced the three pillar concept of **Mission Vision Passion** as an essential 'trifecta' model, providing an explanation of what is, was and had happened at Paradise Rescued from humble, cautious beginnings to the creation of a niche award winning Bordeaux organic wine micro-brand. The three pillars have created an exciting framework for the development of our business. All three pillars have had a major part to offer in relation to the sustainability and success of business.

As I will discuss more later, I regularly see businesses of all sizes that consistently try to shortcut one or more of these pillars as they develop. If you don't know why you are there, where you are going and have no genuine greater interest in the business that you lead or work for, then I struggle to see how that organisation can even function with any level of reasonable performance.

David's "White board" model

Late one afternoon, as I continued to think about the concept, I scribbled up a visual portrayal of the **Mission Vision Passion** model on the white board in my office. As an engineer and passionate visual management / picture advocate, I used a Venn diagram type of approach as I could see potential overlaps (and benefits) between each of the three pillars. What came to me was a much deeper understanding of why the model is so powerful. I saw the interrelation between the pillars in a different light and the gaps, that would exist if one of the pillars were not used.

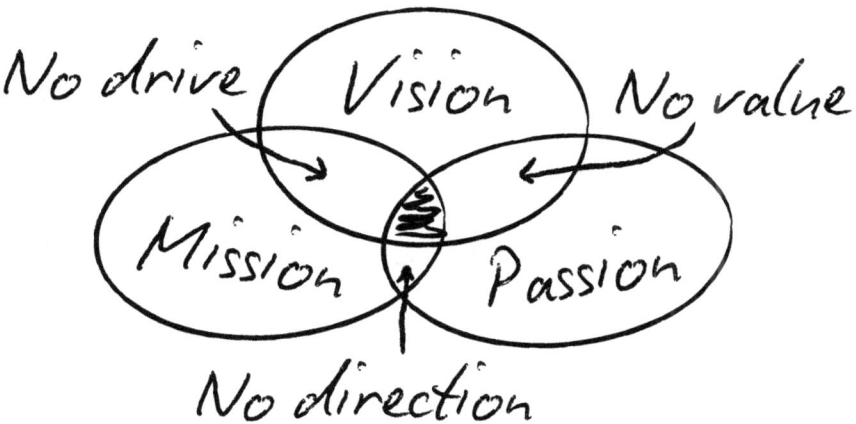

No drive (Vision) No value

Mission Passion

No direction

As I drew the three circles up on the board and labeled them, it was fairly obvious where the sweet spot was – at the intersection or overlap of all three pillars, right in the middle. For my own benefit I shaded that area in as the obvious target area, but then I reflected on what the drawing might also be telling me as I had created three other areas with double (not triple) overlaps. What did that signify?

I studied the model for a good while because I wanted to be sure that I wasn't missing anything in my assessment of what Paradise Rescued had achieved. Did I need a further dimension? Maybe I had one too many?

The shaded area in the middle clearly had it all! I liked that but what was the significance of the other areas and what was missing for an organisation when one of the pillars was not operational?

1. Vision, Mission but no Passion

Let's suppose that an organisation has a Vision and Mission but no Passion. They know why they exist; they know where they are headed but they have no energy, drive nor real desire to make it happen. The bottom line is, they are unlikely to be motivated to make any progress. The net result will be: NO DRIVE.

2. Mission, Passion but no Vision

In this scenario, the team or individual has a Mission and plenty of Passion, but lacks Vision. They will be all fired up and motivated but have nowhere to go. The outcome is that they will rapidly spin in circles without clear forward direction, maintaining the status quo. The future looks uncertain, and they will have NO DIRECTION.

3. Passion, Vision but no Mission

This is a very common model, typically defined by lots of potentially engaged talent working with genuine enthusiasm towards a series of reasonably defined goals, but with no real reason to be there. When there is no purpose to the work and effort being expended, it has NO VALUE.

Through previous career experiences and coaching input many years back, I discovered that a Vision represented as a picture – called (picture)Vision – possessed incredible psychological power that delivered massive leadership influence, advantage, and tangible results in even the harshest of corporate environments. Replication of this, what I call, 'technology' into a smaller but different field of business and sustainability-demands has clearly demonstrated to me (and others) its power to lead, motivate and create significant future change. I will share all of my current thinking, philosophy and application of this (picture)Vision technology in the chapters that follow. It's power to influence through the working, genetic and physical programming of our brains is extremely strong.

Passion sort of found us. The fusion of several similar minds dedicated to sustaining the rural heritage of our village, has drawn in like-minded people who think in a similar way and have injected their own unbelievable passion. This, in turn, has taken not only my passion, attitude and personal commitment to the mission of Paradise Rescued to a higher level, but also that of our loyal dedicated team.

The results of what have been achieved in such a relatively short period of time are very compelling. There is plenty more work to be done and we know we have a long way to travel. Our tiny team has done a lot to achieve two silver Stevie International business awards, one bronze medal for our first ever wine, full organic certification and re-positioning of Cabernet Franc as a premium wine varietal in Bordeaux. I genuinely believe that we are only just getting started. When I taste what is in the barrels year on year, I know that a good part of our model and plan is progressing well, although we're never finished.

The Mission Vision Passion culture will spiral upwards in our organisation as we move further forward, and our team develops further. As they embrace our three-pillar model, the level of achievement will rise further.

Mission Vision Passion. Onwards…

2

Mission vs Vision

It's not a contest but...
Is it important anyway?

I hear a lot of people practically abdicate themselves from any idea of a Mission or Vision. "We work in the real world here, mate! We don't need any of that intangible rubbish, thanks." People often say an iteration of this: "We have a job to do and we simply get on with it. If we do well enough, we get paid and that's as simple as it needs to be."

Does that sound familiar?.

To put it bluntly, *if you don't know why you are where you are nor where you are going, then why are you there at all?*

I understand that you probably need some money to live! If you were there just for the pleasure and no money, then you might as well not be there at all; but does that mean that you just turn up, leave your soul at home and abdicate the next forty to fifty years doing nothing?

I am lucky enough to have lived and worked across a number of countries and continents. I can therefore say with confidence that people everywhere are pretty much the same. Of course, we have different cultures, beliefs, and values; but underneath it all we are human beings striving in some way make sense of our existence. As individuals, or as groups, we all want to achieve something of significance; we all want to succeed and find self-worth in what we do and the value we give to others.

In his best-selling book, [1]*Start With Why* Simon Sinek explains a simple, but effective, three-point formula for corporate and personal success. Sinek's formula works on the principle of the Golden Circle: Why, How and What. Essentially the philosophy proposed is that you need a Why before you find the How and What.

Yes, we go to work to earn money, and yes we love the lunchtime banter about how much we dislike our job and what our plans are once the shift ends, or the work day is done. Invariably, we put more passion into getting out of work than we do when we are there. We spend more time planning our holidays than our lives and careers.

More often that not, when we arrive at the so-called nirvana of retirement, we still don't know what we want to do; at which point, there is only further step to go!

Why spend so many years of our lives being and doing something that we don't enjoy?

Why shouldn't our time be worthwhile and of value?

Much of the same logic can be applied to an organisation or business too. What is its purpose? What is there to accomplish? Where is it heading? What's the plan? Simple questions, right? But can you answer them for the organisation you're in?

[1] Simon Sinek, *Start With Why*, Penguin Press 2011

To pick up on the theme from earlier in the chapter, If you don't know why you are there and if you don't know where you are going, then there is no point to it all, no matter what you're doing, even if you are doing it well.

Mission and Vision are critical to us as individuals and organisations in providing meaning and value; without both, there is no direction nor inspiration. The motivation of money only goes so far and Mission and Vision are at the heart of what leadership is all about.

We all need to know why we are where we are, and where we are going.

Which is which?

I try not to get into arguments at different organisations that I visit and discuss these principles with. I am not sure that I succeed well in this area as I do believe that there is an important difference between a Mission and a Vision. It is important to understand the distinction between them. More often than not, the disagreements I encounter arise from an insufficient understanding of what both a Mission and Vision are. And without some of that fundamental understanding it is really hard to have a meaningful debate nor to use either effectively.

Does it matter if the two get mixed-up and cross interpreted? Perhaps, but not a lot. If you only have one or the other and then you misuse it, it will still work for you but with not as much power as it could. I hope that by the end of this book, you will be able to feel and apply that power. And if you do it correctly, it can achieve amazing results in a manner that fulfills human potential to the maximum.

Mission and Vision are not topics which are generally taught as part of tertiary-level education. As a qualified trained engineer, it was never something that was discussed even in the business management areas of my education, nor was it talked about in formal Business Management school. The focus was much more on management not leadership.

I have been a member of many management teams over my career and it has been fascinating to watch leaders grapple with the difference between Mission and Vision. In many cases, more time is devoted to debating the two, rather than actual thought and effort in successfully developing, setting, and implementing them. After all that time and resource, the results were often recorded on a piece of paper and hung lifelessly in that organisation's reception area.

We do need to differentiate between what constitutes a Mission and what makes up a Vision if we are to have any hope of making and deploying them effectively. We must make the distinction before we can move on and talk about creating a Vision that will inspire or work effectively for an organisation.

Mission – think external

I am going to try and make it simple. In today's Stock Market share-price driven world, generally a Mission is one thing that a company is happy to share at large with the wider community.

Principally it addresses **the WHY question**.

Why does this organisation exist? What is its purpose, its meaning, its cause, significant belief or reason for existence? What does it serve to achieve?

It's that simple. I see different commentators trying to divide this matter into different sub-sections, which only serves to make it more complicated again.

At Paradise Rescued, *everything* starts with our Mission; it describes the reason for our existence and why we are there, doing what we do. As multiple development projects threatened to engulf the rural land and heritage around our family home, Paradise Rescued was created to sustain that rural heritage in Cardan, Bordeaux by exporting fine, organic wine to the world.

And as Simon Sinek reminds us: *"People don't buy WHAT you do, they buy WHY you do it."*

Vision – think internal

There is no harm in sharing a Vision externally, I do it all the time at Paradise Rescued. I don't see any intellectual property loss from doing so. To the contrary, it offers a significant marketing edge by way of an explanation to our customers as to what, how and where we are going.

Most often when I speak with companies and their leaders about their Vision, particularly where they have created a (picture)Vision as opposed to a Vision Statement, they are reluctant to for it to be shared externally to their organisation. I look at the strategic detail prepared in that Vision, I can often see why they don't want it displayed publicly. As I shall show later, when a (picture)Vision is prepared and the magic of the picture based image works well, then indeed the plan will easily convey (or give away if found in competitive hands) the future state, as well as the plan to achieve it.

Vision best addresses **the WHAT question**.

The questions I most often ask, hear and workshop with clients are: "What does it look like?" "If we could see into the future, what could we do achieve?" "If you envision the future, what would you see?" In many ways, it's the perennial question that we all want answered. Why do we read horoscopes or ask a psychic? Because we all want to know what the future brings; we all want to have a picture in our minds of what the future holds because it brings confidence and re-assurance to us. As I discuss in the next chapter, the key word is 'See'. Vision is all about what we see, as it's all based around our sight. It's not an accident that we use that word specifically to describe what we are looking for.

Vision is an internal tool, but if you can confidently use it externally with your customers and other stakeholders, then it adds great power to your communications while strongly reinforcing the message of your Mission. Conversely, if your Mission cannot be shared with the world outside of your organisation, then I would have to question its value at all; and I suspect that if it does remain locked internally, it will not have as much motivational power within your team.

Part B

The Power of Pictures

3

Introduction to Visual Management

Senses are our data-input devices to our brain that enable us to assess the relative significance of different parameters in our personal world. We use the data we receive and interpret it as the basis for our decision making, and self protection.

We traditionally think of *five primary human senses*, namely:

- Sight - Hearing - Taste - Smell - Touch

We also have other minor senses such as temperature, pain, balance, etc. As part of our human physiology, these extra senses are intrinsically linked to our human psychology; how we behave, act, and react to any given situation depends on how our brains interpret the data provided to us through our senses.

When we think of human performance, it is clearly better to work **with** our human psychology to get the most from our sensory inputs. By trying to work **against** what our senses tell us is very difficult and usually results in a poor outcome, hence, we learn to work **with** them in order to achieve the results we want.

When leading people, ourselves included under the category of self leadership, we learn that it is better to work **with** people if we want to achieve anything. The more we learn about, and understand human psychology and behaviour, the more successful we will most likely be when working with our fellow human beings. The same applies to senses. If we deploy the most effective human sense, we can expect to maximise the chances of success.

Here's a different but very simple illustration, as demonstrated by our relationship with 'man's best friend', our dogs. If we want to influence a dog, what do we do? Tempt the dog with food! Why? Because they eat to survive and they have one very incredible almost overwhelming sense – smell! In many cases, dogs become almost hypnotised when the possibility of eating food is imminent, they will stay close at hand and become instantly obedient. A dog's sense of smell and overriding desire to eat in order to sustain their well being dominates their behaviour.

It's easy to try and differentiate ourselves from other species by labelling them as animals (and hence, of lower apparent intellectual ability) while seeing ourselves as superior, more intelligent creatures above these physiological influences. A quick review of the television evening news should be enough to bring us back to earth and provide a reminder that we are all animals and that the so-called intelligence benefit we are born with as humans is sadly wasted.

In a digital age, we like to believe that the 'data decides', well, it certainly helps. Indeed we can and often do abdicate our decision-making power to a computer processor, but in most cases our decision-making power is derived from inside of us, based on what our senses are telling us about something. We use phrases such as 'my gut tells me' or 'in my heart' as a reflection of our humanity and every major investment decision we make as an organisation, or an individual, still relies on an internal human component of confidence.

What is important, is to realise that our senses play a significant part of our decision-making processes and, therefore, to specifically decide not to use our senses or abdicate the decision-making to some other power will take us down a route of just 'going with the flow', heading where we are already going. Leadership requires that we do make a decision and set a direction for the future.

So, given that we have five primary senses, how can we make best use of one or all of them? Which one of those five is the most effective? Which one do we use most often? Which one is the most important to us?

In my seminars and talks, I always do a quick survey of the audience as to which sense they rate the most highly. In almost all cases, the overwhelming majority give their answer as Sight – our ability to see. Obviously, the response varies from person to person, but this is by far the most common answer. Sight is critical to our self preservation at the basic 'needs' level, right through to the higher requirements of an individual; it is critical in gauging how close or far we are from danger, assessing whether our food will be safe and nutritional (no matter how good it smells) and your assessment of the person opposite you as a potential partner.

We react, assess, analyse and respond based on the data we get from our senses. What we see matters a lot; it's level of importance also plays a big role in our psychology and how we behave. Aided by the advancement in digital technology, Social Media has dramatically altered our world at a huge pace. Even if you are not a big fan, nor participant, the impact is undeniably significant and some of that has been very positive, while other parts not so good.

The best test would be to send a word only text message to a group of friends describing an event compared to a picture of that same event. Which one will get the greatest reaction? Almost invariably, the picture will get the greater reaction by a significant margin. Why do we prefer to enjoy sport on television rather than radio? Why does a face to face meeting work so much better than a telephone call or email? Simply because we can adsorb so much more data and sense what is happening so much better through people's visual responses and reactions. In other words we can actually see (and feel) what is going on!

Sight adds a massive quantity and quality of content to the data that we receive into our brains on a second by second basis. I will talk about this 'data' in more detail in the next chapter, but I think it is easy to understand how much power it gives us as a sense. A significant part of our lives – mobility, perceptions and greater comprehension of our world comes through sight. People who do not have this sense or have lost it can compensate in other ways, but none of that is easy, given its power and richness in terms of light, dark, colour, human expression, and overall images that it can convey.

There are many examples at Paradise Rescued that I can relate to. Wine is very much a sight, taste, and smell subject. One of the best examples I can think of, and that I use every day, is the westerly view across the Cabernet Franc vineyard towards the 12th century church on the hill opposite; the view is exactly what our friends and neighbours in Cardan, Bordeaux wake up to and enjoy every day. The picturesque view is the inspiration and sustainable motivation for the existence, and day-to-day pursuit of excellence at Paradise Rescued. When we welcome new customers, team members, media, or anyone who has never previously been to visit us, we take them to the high point in the vineyard looking down along the rows of vines leading their eyes up and across the uninterrupted view over the small church.

Their reaction is always the same. "Wow, that's so beautiful, now I can see why you do this business. Thank you." It's that simple. The countryside in France is breathtaking and has thousands of similar beautiful views, but that particular view as seen through the eyes of our community and by visitors for the first time has specific meaning. Words, sound, smell, and taste are irrelevant. The empowerment, inspiration, and motivation that come from that view, that picture view is overwhelming, leading people to volunteer time and resources in a positively disproportionate manner like I have never seen.

> *"A picture is worth a thousand words."*
> Unknown

The question is how best to harness the power that our sense of sight and a picture gives us. And how can we use it to create Vision.

4

Reticular
Activating
System

Just imagine if we were able to download an app that we could use to help guide us towards what we wanted! Just think what it would be like to be equipped 24/7 with a human tool that could sieve out the good stuff that we wanted from all the rest of the data and "stuff" coming at us continually. Wouldn't it be amazing if we could put that tool to work to work for us in the way we wanted?

Our most important app

The very good news is that we are all equipped with such an amazing app! It comes free of charge. It doesn't even need to be downloaded. We are all born with it and we use on a daily basis. In most cases we are unaware of its existence and potential to help our lives. If the settings are incorrect and not understood, it can most likely have a detrimental effect. If well focused and given the right settings and stimulus, it can be one of our most powerful human assets.

It's called the Reticular Activating System or RAS as I will call it throughout the rest of this book. It's part of our brain and we all have one! Without it, we wouldn't function at all!

As with so many of our human assets, the vast majority of us do not appreciate that we have the skills and potential that we are given at birth. Similarly, whether we choose to make use of our in-built advantage and maximise its potential or merely ignore it doesn't alter that fact that it is there and available. So the lesson is therefore to find the RAS and ask it to work for us. And not against us!

This is not a book for budding brain surgeons, neuroscience or neurobiology! Although I do find it noteworthy that there is relatively little written and readily available on the subject of the RAS. But maybe that's the key point? We are fascinated in understanding how our minds work but almost totally disinterested in applying the science to improve communication between human beings and the pursuit of a better world. We use up way too much mental capacity in working out how to hurt fellow human beings than to help them. Let's see if we can do a little it to change that.

In this chapter I will show why understanding where the neurons flow is less important than the impact the RAS has on our psychology, how we see the world and then potentially how we can more effectively influence the lives of others through our personal or group leadership. At the end of the day, we are here to talk leadership and how to present a powerful compelling Vision.

In our everyday lives, we all use electrical devices. We learn very quickly that if we want light, we flick the switch on the wall and bingo, we get light! It may be nice to know how electricity is generated and distributed to us, but for most of us the learning of where the switch is and what can do is sufficient. It's the same for our RAS.

The RAS is a part of our brains. It lives at the back of our brains somewhere near the top of our spinal chords. All of our senses (weirdly excluding smell) are wired through the RAS. All of the information that we receive into our conscious mind goes through the RAS. In fact it is the RAS that decides which information to let in and which to discard. It therefore acts as a filter or gatekeeper for our brain. With so much information being fed in from our sensory systems, the brain has to be able to decide what to process inwards and what to discard.

The RAS is on duty 24/7, even when we sleep during which time it mostly lets us do exactly that. Unless something very important – such as an emergency arises – in which case it sends a message to the brain to wake us up. If you have become very focused on something, like buying a red car, suddenly we are more likely to start seeing red cars everywhere. The number of red cars hasn't changed in an instant but our human mental awareness has been given a higher priority by our RAS. So effectively the RAS will go to work on finding the data we are seeking whilst rejecting everything else that is less important.

We often talk about the Law of Attraction – that is the ability to attract into our lives whatever we are focusing on. More often than not, we believe that the Law of Attraction is some kind of superpower that certain positive thinking individuals have invented in order to focus their thinking and realise their future achievements. Proponents of this believe passionately in it whilst the naysayers discount it on the basis of the philosophy being just a load of fluffy mental nonsense.

Funnily enough, as we understand the power of the RAS, both the believers and detractors are correct. Henry Ford has been credited with the phrase "Whether you think you can or whether you think you can't, you are absolutely right." What we believe is what is imprinted on our RAS filter. So if we think the world is a negative messed-up place working to conspire against us, then guess what? Our RAS will pull out the data from the world around us that supports our internal belief and it will look exactly that way.

Interestingly it's the same world and often the same circumstances that leads a different mindset to believe a totally different approach is possible and that the world is what we make it. And one that is abundant with opportunity?

Isn't this bizarre? Yes, indeed it is! But as I wrote earlier: don't worry about the neurons and science of why this happens. I challenge you to work with the understanding and new knowledge of what the RAS does and then how to put that use to work *for* you rather than *against* you. Two critical learnings come from this knowledge of the RAS:-

Firstly, that the RAS is our primary data and senses filter. And as a filter we can decide what to put on that filter to tell it what to pass through. Imagine this all happening in slow motion rather than the rapid pace at which the RAS normally has to work. Let's picture each one of those bits of data coming in from our senses. As it gets to the RAS, the filter asks the piece of data to show its identity pass. The RAS scans the pass and checks whether that data is going to be allowed in. If the data is on the approved list, it can pass onwards to the brain. If it's not, it will be rejected and forgotten. So if we can programme or set the criteria by which data can pass to our brains, we have a powerful human psychological tool to work for us.

The RAS is our multi-sensory data filter. We can tell it what we want it to recognise by what we expose to the most.

Secondly, it is up to us as to how we can set up that RAS programme of criteria. We can choose to abdicate that responsibility in a manner that can positively impact our family, world, business or whatever we have a passion to do. Alternatively, we can choose to let our belief system and RAS take on a set of values and data selection criteria that will *exclude* what we need to achieve what we like to have, see, do and be. All of which may negatively impact on other people.

This means that we have the power of choice over the selection criteria of our RAS. We can choose and therefore decide how to programme it to our advantage, rather than disadvantage. This therefore comes down to a set of decisions about what we want to do, who we want to do it with and in what environment we choose to place ourselves. In a world that is now so rich in its media, we have to be increasingly more selective than ever before on where we focus. Remember bad news sells best. And as we can see in our everyday lives, there is a lot of it out there. The more we focus on something – good or bad - the greater the chance that we will accept the data that re-enforces the belief.

When you approach it in this way, it is easy to see that the Law of Attraction is not a spiritual gift. We all have the app that makes it work for us. It's just a question of the (different) manner in which we have applied the settings. In other words, whether we have decided on the good things or bad things in life, on positive outcomes or negative outcomes, our brain (via the Reticular Activating System) will figure out how to do it.

Let's put it to work.

Your RAS takes what you choose to focus on and creates a filter for it. It then sifts through the incoming data and presents only the pieces that are important to you. All of this happens without you noticing, of course. The RAS programs itself to work in your favor without you actively doing anything. Pretty awesome, right?

In the same way, the RAS seeks information that validates your beliefs. It filters the world through the parameters you give it, and your *beliefs* shape those parameters. If you think you are bad at giving speeches, you probably will be. If you believe you work efficiently, you most likely do. The RAS helps you see what you want to see and in doing so, influences your actions.

Some people suggest that you can train your RAS by taking your subconscious thoughts and marrying them to your conscious thoughts. This is called 'setting your intent.' This basically means that if you focus hard on your goals, your RAS will reveal the people, information and opportunities that help you achieve them.

If you care about positivity, for example, you will become more aware of and seek positivity. If you really want a pet turtle and set your intention on getting one, you'll tune in to the right information that helps you do that.

When you look at it this way, The Law of Attraction doesn't seem so mystical. Focus on the bad things and you will invite negativity into your life. Focus on the good things and they will come to you, because your brain is seeking them out. It's not magic, it's your Reticular Activating System influencing the way you see the world around you.

"What you see is what you get" runs the traditional saying. If sight is our most important and useful sense, how can we put that to best use to help us achieve what we want in business, life and for the sustainability of our planet?

5

What You See is What You Get

We have established that there are two natural human powers – the power of our sight and our Reticular Activating System (RAS). Both are continually working for us. For most people, our sight is the dominant sense feeding our RAS with data that decides which parts to use and discards the rest. These two mechanisms work for us, or against us, as we choose and are inbuilt as part of our human psychology. Whether we like them or not; whether we use them or not, they work as part of us. So, it is our choice whether to deploy them for our benefit – and hopefully others too – or otherwise. But it is our own individual choice and decision – not someone else's!

So, what if there is indeed a way of combining these two human powers together that could lead us to better human performance and achievement as individuals, teams, groups or families? Could they work together in some way that could give us more predictable results?

Yes, they can!

Combining two powerful advantages

The combined learning of the two previous chapters presents the following summary facts:

1. Sight is our most powerful sense

2. Our RAS filters data from our human senses and can be programmed to specifically select the data that we wish to see.

The conclusion therefore is that data presented to us visually will have the greatest influence on our RAS and brain. And that if we can consistently present a coherent and emotionally strong visual message, i.e. a picture in front of our eyes (and hence our RAS), it's impact can have a powerful impact on how we see our world and what data we look for and take in.

Let's break it down a little further. That was a very short paragraph summary of the first section of this book. If you can grasp this concept sufficiently and then apply, it can give you a lot of potential leverage to create your / our future word, be it family, organisation, community or business. The key to doing that starts with a picture.

In this digital age, we have learned to use pictures and visual media to the maximum. And yet, when we want to lead and motivate ourselves or a larger group to achieve something more lasting, we forget what works best!

President JF Kennedy presented the USA with a Vision when speaking to congress in 1961 telling them that "this nation should commit itself to achieving the goal, before this decade is out, of landing a man on the moon and returning him safely to the Earth." It succeeded because the concept or vision was very simple even if achieving that goal was not. I suspect every American looked at the moon in a different way from that moment onwards. Our RAS was impacted.

Most visions are not always that straightforward. So, when a leader gives a 'vision speech' or posts a 'vision statement' on the wall of the company at reception, the vision fails to resonate and inspire. It does not leave a significant impression on our RAS so the natural data filtering process that goes on there will largely ignore the message. For a vision to be achieved it requires everyone to understand the direction. A few words in a talk or as part of a framed document on the wall does not cut it. We want everyone to have the same common picture in their minds and on their RAS for it to have sufficient power to filter out the necessary data and ideas to bring it to fruition.

Put more bluntly, so-called vision statements and one-off motivational leadership talks do not succeed. Why, because a clear consistent message does not get imprinted onto the RAS filter and it won't go to work to achieve the results that that group or organisation want. We have to work with our strengths and human psychology.

We need a (picture)Vision.

My observation however is that despite the widespread broadcasting of visual media – external visualisation – when it comes to internal visualisation, there is a huge opportunity to be realised.

Let's get it on paper

If sight is the key and spoken or written words alone don't effectively work, what is the solution?

Draw your vision on paper.

Create a (picture)Vision – an image of what your life, organisation, factory, team will look like in five or more years from now. That is a compelling picture or image that represents and depicts the required future of that group. Put it onto paper where it is clearly visible and frequently seen by everyone involved in achieving that vision.

The process of creating a (picture)Vision is more powerful than throwing down a few words on a piece of paper. The power comes from engaging our minds in the process of visualising what the future will look like. And that process itself impacts on the RAS and the future data or messages that the brain will filter in as time progresses.

The details of how to do it and deploy it come later on in Section C.

Taking the concept to a new level

Using visions and visualisation is nothing new. They all try to work off the same principle – namely to imprint a reference image on the filter of our RAS against which all the incoming data is compared such that our brains can then be triggered to act on those things that are important. The specific change is how we portray that vision to our RAS it in order to get better results and increase the chances of a positive successful outcome.

Here are some examples where visualisation is readily used...

Sport performance

Anyone who lives in and around Melbourne Australia will find it hard to ignore the passion and culture that is "footy". Australian Rules football is a game that is uniquely Australian and has a concentration of cultural intensity in and around that city. Despite Melbourne being an intensely sport focused place, footy stands above all other sports as the number one supported game.

At the end of this last season, one of the finalist teams was the Collingwood Magpies, a team that creates instant division within the city football culture. They play in black and white stripe colours and whether you like them or not, is a similar black or white decision. They have a large "competitive" fan base that pulls in all parts of Melbourne's culture. After a few seasons of rebuilding but sliding results, they rebounded against all predictions and found themselves in the Grand Final. Which they subsequently lost to the West Coast Eagles from Perth.

One of their rising stars is a 24-year-old Brodie Grundy, who rose to prominence in the sport during the season leading up to the final. Just prior to the final, the media woke up to his story.

Grundy says: *"The belief that the group has is really strong. Visualisation is a really important part of that for me, so that's how I go about it – believing that it's possible and then chasing it."*

But Grundy isn't unique in the elite sports field. Other world class athletes such as Novak Djokovic, Jonny Wilkinson, Michael Jordan and Michael Phelps all promote and practice some kind of mental visualisation technique as a part of their *daily* success routines.

Business performance

In business the use of visions – more often statements than pictures – is not uncommon. If used or deployed correctly and openly shared with others, a future concept or perceived picture of what that business will look like sometime in the future can be realized.

In 2016, TD Bank New Jersey shared its results of having surveyed more than 1100 small businesses and 500 individuals. They found that:

• Almost two-thirds of small business owners believe that visualizing goals helps them map and develop their business plans.

• One in five small business owners used a vision board or other visual representation when starting their business; 76% of those business owners said that today their business is where they envisioned it would be when they started it.

- Eighty-two percent of small business owners that used a vision board from the get-go reported that they have accomplished more than half the goals they included on that board.

My own work at Paradise Rescued and in other larger public business units would echo the results here. Working hard on creating a vision significantly increases the chances of a successful outcome.

Personal performance

The use of visualisation technology is not exclusively the domain of elite sports teams and business. All organisations consist of people. Those people are the ones that make results happen. And a company or organisation is a collection of those people. If they all believe in a shared vision, like Brodie Grundy states above, then significant strength and direction of purpose can be achieved.

As individuals, usually operating without a coach, we use another technique. It's called Goal Setting. We set ourselves a goal to achieve something, ranging from a lifetime holiday to having a family to getting a new job or whatever. And in order to do that, we normally apply a lot of effort and focus to that desired goal that we have set ourselves to do.

The key here is the word focus. As human beings when we focus on something very specific, we research, study and imagine what it will be like when we have achieved that special thing. In so doing, the lens on our RAS is increasingly imprinted with impressions of what that goal will look like and goes to work to help make it happen. We sometimes try to encourage the process along by putting individual pictures on the fridge door as an example. PS – please do not put your bills there, otherwise you will simply get more (of what you put in front of your senses!).

Seeing really is believing

The examples above highlight a very important learning for

us humans. That if we can "see" something in our minds, a future desired outcome or state, our minds will usually find the required data from everything going on it our worlds around us to bring it into reality.

As I have previously written in *It's Not About the Dirt*, we are often unprompted to use the expression "I will believe that when I see it". It's normally spoken in a negative and sarcastic tone to help put down someone else's tough-minded optimistic wish. By creating visions in a way that our brains and RAS combined can put to positive achievement, we can start to believe them before reality overtakes us again dissuades us from that exciting future. To foster and fuel that belief we need to create compelling visions that will emotionally connect with us and imprint a picture on our RAS filter that will pick out the opportunity data. What you see is what you get!

Creating a Vision, Visualisation or enVisioning success for good is simply using the power of or minds in a creative natural way. As I wrote previously in Chapter three, we all have the natural psycho-technology already in our human DNA and psychology. The app doesn't require a download or a credit card. It is already available for us to use and harvest.

We are looking to create a clear mental picture of a future condition, state, assets, culture, organisation, etc. In order to create that clear mental picture we need to consistently and regularly put an emotionally compelling physical picture of that future regularly in our sight such that it will become part of our RAS filter. We need to create a (picture)Vision.

Now comes the fun bit: how to do it! And how to best use it! Let's look at how we can harness our ability to make our future happen on purpose!

> *"You can't be what you can't see"*
> Sally Capp Lord Mayor Melbourne.

Part C

Creating a (picture)Vision

6

Setting up Some Rules

Knowing what it is/what it isn't

I want to stress here up front that drawing a (picture)Vision is not a five minute brainstorming exercise. It requires good solid thought, study and reflection. And probably several attempts to get it right. Quite often I am asked to go and help an organisation for a 'few minutes' to get them on the 'right track'. Don't fall for the usual management team trap that it's on this month's agenda to 'tick off' the Vision (statement). If you put very little real effort in up front, I can almost guarantee the results you will get. If you end up with an incomplete plan on your vision, you will most likely achieve *exactly* that due to the power of your mind and RAS combined. Be very careful what you ask for!

If you are serious about designing an empowering future and

Vision, be equally committed in your time and thinking to achieving your future state.

Put it down on paper!

I know this is the digital age. I understand. I am writing this book on my laptop and not with a quill pen on parchment paper! But I implore you to start your (picture)Vision on a piece of paper. We are increasingly seeing the arrival of tablet style notepads with digital pens which will also help as changes will be more easy to adjust instantly. The key thing is to get the ideas down and recorded. It has to be a picture (or symbol)! Captured ideas and innovation are not enough. It is all focused around "What does it look like?"

When I run workshops with organisations helping them create their futures, I make them start with a piece of A3 paper, some colourful pens and marker pens. And then ask the participants to simply draw their ideas as a picture onto the paper as they come into their head. The visual component is the key to success here and influencing our RAS.

As I tell the story in my first book *From Cabbage Patch to Cabernet Franc*, whilst working on another corporate strategic project with my coach Sue Gregory, we discussed the future concept – and picture – of Paradise Rescued on several occasions over a drink or meal. During many of those sessions, we found ourselves scribbling on the paper table covers as the ideas came in. The process of transferring ideas into pictures was taking place and in so doing, laying down the foundations of the future Vision on my RAS.

In one of those sessions, we talked more about the mission of the future company and tried to envision what was its role. The future of our corner of the village of Cardan, Bordeaux together with its rural heritage was on the line. We started to see the need to rescue what I saw – and still see today – as a small corner of (my) paradise. That's how the name Paradise Rescued was created.

The ideas that go down on paper for you and your teams will be the ones that ultimately transfer to the subsequent draft or final (picture)Vision. At that stage it may be appropriate to have someone smarten it up. At Paradise Rescued, I redrew the images as a coherent picture using an engineering tool called Visio. That worked for me, but you can choose how you want to do that. Or not at all – you may elect to stay in native type format.

Don't forget that the first (picture)Vision you create will act as the first draft and basis for the next period. It's a continually growing picture. It most likely won't be perfect first time around. It doesn't matter – it can be improved later. Get the pictures down. The power is in the picture.

Set a future timeframe

Setting a decent future time frame is critical. I strongly advise a decent long term. The whole idea is to create a strong future direction. Five years is a good period over which meaningful change, action can occur and value is created.

We all see way too much short-term focus with stock markets, remuneration, quick fix and influence ideas. As a society in general, we seem to increasingly want it all now. Programming and focusing our RAS is not a five-minute event leading to immediate results. Like fine wine, cheese and relationships, it always takes much longer to create something of lasting value. And when working in teams and groups of people, enduring change takes time to be imputed and for the direction to be aligned towards a new future.

Include your values

This is a very challenging aspect of your (picture)Vision work! But an extremely important part. Again, I see lots of different – often half hearted – attempts to lead organisations through the poor deployment of values. Values need to clear and visible to everyone as well as continually communicated throughout the organisation they relate to. Too often, I see a few words on a wall, a quick leader speech and video put out there in the hope that the values will be lapped up with hungry enthusiasm.

Armed now with your understanding of how our minds / RAS work together, you can quickly see how the conventional use or launch of values into a group is unlikely to be successful. These processes take time to strongly influence our minds and paint new images onto our RAS. Which helps to also explain why culture change is often slow and sometimes impossible. One speech or a few words on the wall don't work. Until the picture in our minds changes, we won't adjust either!

Try and capture the values into the (picture)Vision. Write them initially as words but work to integrate them in some way as part of the Vision. Try to avoid whole sentences and instead perhaps just use one or two words if you need to as part of a visual setting.

In the first chapter of my second book *It's Not About the Dirt,* I wrote about the impact that this process had on Paradise Rescued in just its second year of operation. In the first two years of production, our Cabernet Franc fermentation was carried out in one single vat. The 2011 vintage was very warm with an early harvest which when combined with a single oversized vat led to some technical difficulties. The result was that the wine would not be saleable at the price / value point we were seeking to achieve.

I remember the phone call from our winemaker Albane offering me various options or swap deals such that we might have a saleable product of any kind. As I took the call, I looked up at the Paradise Rescued (picture)Vision on the wall at my office desk. Our values are depicted inside a bottle and at the top of that list is "Quality and Excellence". What had occurred in our winery clearly did not meet those values. The decision was easy; there was no doubt nor compromise. The poor quality wine had to dumped and we started all over again in 2012. Our single vat was replaced with smaller more flexibly sized equipment and our wine quality has taken a step-change upwards from that time forward.

Use colour and lots of it!

You want the brain to be impacted. That's for the same reason that the media guys try to 'shock' us with every news release. Bad news or dramatic news gets our attention in and around the minute by minute constancy of the data our RAS and brain receives. Now I am not advising you to use shock tactics but I am encouraging you to use bold colour as that will more readily catch the attention of your RAS and brain.

Be clear, bold and colourful. The simpler the message, image the better. Colour is a great way to differentiate something and make it stand out and therefore be more easily noticed by our senses. The best way to experience the impact of this is to look at an old black and white photograph or drawing and then seeing the same thing remastered in colour.

If colour didn't matter why don't we all still buy black Model T Ford cars?

Colour adds dimension and emotion, which is turn creates internal passion. Bright green grass is much more appealing to the senses than dead winter grass. Red wine in a glass has infinitely more impact than water in a similar container?

Add in top metrics.

What gets measured gets done! Right? Yes indeed, well thought out goals are good. This will also lead later into correctly setting up annual target setting and monthly / weekly results dashboards. Again, plenty of thought needs to go into this part of the (picture)Vision. It is not sufficient to simply write down some figure that you have snatched out of thin air that takes you from last in class to world's best. Or to add a profitability and shareholder value target that is so unrealistic that it will immediately generate your next new competitor.

Every one of us has seen those business plans, government forecasts, etc that turn up very positively at the end of the plan period. As a former grass hockey player and observer of these plans over time, we call these the 'hockey stick' effect. It all suddenly goes miraculously right!

Profitability and financial outcomes are usually the result of having done a whole series of other operational activities well. If you do those things well, set tough minded KPIs for those performance metrics and achieve them, the financials will most probably follow. So, think and focus on the leading indicators that will follow through on to the business results at that level of performance deserves.

Be bold, strong and courageous.

Most of my life, I have been accused in big business of being too optimistic. I have certainly learnt over time that I am more likely to achieve better outcomes by having a positive approach to leadership and management than a negative one. And the same goes for a forward-looking plan or (picture)Vision. If you don't believe that your business, group or organisation has or can have a successful future, then there is very little point in being a part of it. If you are simply there for the pay or prestige, rather than developing its future, then you are in the wrong place.

The challenge however is to find the right balance between empty-headed dreamy ideas and a challenging achievable set of future goals. I call this space 'tough-minded optimism'. As Henry Ford famously said once: if you believe you can or you believe you can't, you are right! As leaders, our role is to work out what can be achieved and to take others on the journey to make it happen.

The road ahead will not be easy. Creating something of value requires bold decisions, strong persistent leadership and courageous moments that embrace humanity to achieve that extra something. If it's too easy to achieve, it most likely won't be worth it.

I challenge you to push the boundaries. Go where no one has been before but make sure that you can see something of a road or plan to get there. If your (picture)Vision is uninspiring and does not create the passion and environment where innovation can flourish, it hasn't done its' job. If it's completely unrealistic such that no one can see how it could be achieved, then it similarly won't inspire.

Now we have set up the rules, let's start to put it all into action.

"Words on walls are worthless"
David Stannard, The Vision Guy

Additional resources to assist you in the creation and further development of your own (picture)Vision can be found at www.thevisionguy.com.au/trifectaresources

7

From a Dream, to Paper, to Reality

A (picture)Vision is the key stepping stone between a dream and reality. When well thought out, drawn up and correctly displayed, a (picture)Vision becomes the strong mental mind map and picture that will take a great idea (or set of ideas) and help pull together the energy and resources to make it into existence.

As I talked about in *It's Not About the Dirt*, almost everyone has a dream or good idea at some time. We often talk about those ideas as dreams because more often than not, they have a very short life. We frequently ridicule our friends and family members' wild sudden ideas as 'that's just a fanciful dream'.

Everything that we use today, we take for granted on a daily basis. But once upon a time, it was just a dream. Amazing ideas are ruined and lost every second of the day by other people who discount them. The pressures, our endless activity and the learned helplessness of daily life can easily push those dreams out of our heads.

Here's a few examples of big dreams that didn't die:

- Julius Caesar invaded Britain
- Karl Benz invented the first motor car.
- Amelia Earhart flew the Atlantic solo
- Travis Kalanick and Garrett Camp founded Uber

To bring a dream to life, to make it happen, to convert it into reality requires a lot of persistence and perspiration by the person who first thought of it and wants to make it something real out of it. It takes a lot of individual leadership, determination and personal courage to make something good happen.

I see a lot of people who talk about making your dreams come true. But unless you have a plan or a bridge to join that dream to reality, the chance of crossing the raging torrents of the success river is unlikely. We need a tool that facilitates the journey. We need a way to capture the good ideas as soon as we can and in a format that empowers the best individual – and group – motivation to achieve the goal.

A (picture)Vision is that plan - that link and that bridge across the difficult period of dream destruction and obsolescence. It is a simple tool to use that can automatically plan and align our minds to go to work on achieving reality.

Leadership and people power

There are many models of leadership available in today's media rich world. Sadly, the ones that we most commonly see are those of arrogance, dictatorial behaviour and self ego. There is sometimes a place for "strong" leadership in that sense and difficult decisions do indeed have to be made and followed through. Quite often though we misinterpret and complain bitterly about this kind of leadership.

In reality we all are, or can be, leaders. We all have the ability and capability if we simplify what leadership is all about. Leadership is about being prepared to make something of value happen and influence others into helping.

Nothing changes or happens by itself. An idea requires a leader to champion it and make it happen through and with other people. A powerful way to communicate, articulate a goal clearly, create a consistency of purpose and minimise possible misinterpretation is by creating a picture – a (picture)Vision of what it is we are seeking to achieve.

The (picture)Vision is what creates that positive pull and tension to bring the future into reality. We first have to create a clear compelling image in our own head and then in the minds of those who follow and help us. That's the power of leadership.

In an organisation, the greater the number of people with that same clear picture, the more rapid and empathic will be the achievement of a common goal. The key comes down to defining what it looks like and how to communicate that to those we lead or choose to follow us of the outcome we are seeking to create. When our team is aligned – they have the same picture of success – then the power of implementation can become exponential.

Getting your (picture)Vision started

The key to action and making anything happening is getting started. The first step is often the most challenging and fearful. The one advantage of a creating a (picture)Vision is that the process outlined in the previous chapter is relatively straight forward.

Here is a quick plan to get your group started:-

1. Organise Paper A1 flipcharts – the giant Post-It kind than can be safely be attached to a wall after drawing are great. In a tight workshop environment A3 paper can also work well.

2. Provide lots of pens, textas, markers and highlighters to draw images and colourful stuff on the paper.

3. Make available standard 3 inch square Post-its are useful also to capture other ideas / changes.

4. Use groups of no more than 10 people – preferably smaller if space and logistics permits. 5 is a perfect number where

everyone can step up and showcase their picture drawing talents.

5. For a first effort, use 45 minutes maximum discussion and drawing time. If working with a number of sub groups, it may be useful to stop and have each small group present what they have drawn and thought. Let the ideas grow slowly over a break and if needs be, come back and draw a second draft.

6. Draw what you see in your mind. Draw images of what you want the future to look like. Be innovative, make it fun and use lots of colour!

In producing a (picture)Vision, there is a fine balance between contribution, empowerment and ownership. A full bottom-up process will not work. I strongly believe in everyone having some input – so far as is practical. Everyone in an organisation brings different skills, values and insights. But senior leadership is responsible for pulling all of that energy into one coherent plan – your (picture)Vision. It is not a consensus plan; decisions have to be made on priorities and direction. The leaders, in conjunction with all levels of the organisation, are responsible for pulling that together. And decision making.

Self-reflection and shower time

One of the great temptations, as I reflected earlier in the book, is our ever-increasing desire for everything to get faster and quicker. A (picture)Vision should most likely cover a decent future time space of say five years. It is important therefore not to fall into the trap of thinking that something seemingly simple yet powerful as a (picture)Vision can be achieved very quickly. Plan your time and approach to achieving the right outcome.

A lot of quality thinking must be put into to getting it as right as possible at the time of drawing. Sure, not everything can be perfect when you are trying to create the future. And similarly, the environment around you won't play out in the exact manner that you wish. But if you put in significant mental effort to getting right up front, I am confident you get rewards at the outcome.

The quantity of successful results from your (picture)Vision will reflect the quality of your initial input.

I encourage you to take some quality time, to develop several drafts and to look at them consistently over a few weeks to make sure you are comfortable with the picture you are developing. In the process of looking at the draft your RAS will quickly assimilate the picture into your mind and start the sub-conscious testing and analysis. These processes happen over time, when you are showering, sleeping, relaxing, taking a walk etc. This self-reflection is critical and helps to either improve those parts of the Vision that need further clarity and improvement or they will crystallise the images firmly into your RAS and mind.

You will also see over time, how your constant sharing, vision casting, presentation and review of your (picture) Vision continues this process of improvement and focus.

Making it personal – ownership

One of the reasons I talked above about who and how much involvement or buy-in other team members should have is the fact that *someone has to own* the Vision.

Typically, the owner is the GM, CEO and leader of that group to which the (picture)Vision relates. The leader must take responsibility for the final picture, its development, deployment and action planning. This aligns also with what I wrote earlier about leadership. Passion, commitment and communication are key here and we will talk in the next chapter about how to do this well and get the Vision deep into the organisation.

The leader will have to make decisions about the content of the final (picture)Vision. This is a decision-making activity and its delegation is not an option. Other team members and team leaders need to contribute but ultimately the top leader of that group or organisation must decide and demonstrate their ownership.

If the leader wants to see the (picture)Vision come to life, she/he knows that they have to be the number one champion of it. They have to commit their passion to it in order to make it succeed.

If the leader makes it personal, the organisation can see it in the tonality and passion of that individual. The (picture)Vision will gain commitment and buy-in from the organisation.

Flexibility

One word of caution on your (picture)Vision. It won't be perfect. Predicting uncontrollable variables in the world, business, politics, universe in general is an imperfect science. Give yourself some room to manoeuvre by not making it all so rigid that the slightest deviation in external or internal events makes your beautiful new (picture)Vision unrealistic.

Always remember that the goal is to develop a tough-minded optimistic picture of your future. At the same time, endless paralysis by analysis and indecision will not.

If you don't create your future, someone else will create it for you! So, make you best current estimate, make a plan and get some momentum happening. The worst mistake that we can make in life is to not make up our minds and *commit*. A decision not to decide is still a decision.

Make it live

You will have set in place a key directional plan for your business. Use that plan. If it has a five year time horizon, make sure that it gets refreshed and updated at the end of the time line.

I have a story to close this chapter on. In one of my plant leadership roles, I remember we were reaching the end of that facility's (picture)Vision time horizons. When chatting with one of my first line supervisors after lunch one day he asked me "David, where is the new vision? Do we have one?" Clearly, he was interested in both his and the plant's future. I went on to explain that I had been gathering input for the revised (picture)Vision and I was nearly ready to launch the next five-year vision. "That's great, David. It is very reassuring to see our future, to see where we are heading. Thank you."

Let's work now on putting your (picture)Vision to active work and getting the organisational creativity and everyone's RAS focused and filtering.

8

Bringing it to Life

So now we have our (picture)Vision, how we get everyone else to join in. To align, to participate, to innovate, to create, to make it come alive. I think we all recognise that the power of many can achieve more than a select few individuals. No one person has all the skills, knowledge, network and ideas to bring about significant change and creation of a unique project or successful organisation.

It used to be something that supposedly successful and rich entrepreneurs quote to the world as a measure of their personal brilliance that they are 'self-made' heroes. In every case of self-proclaimed brilliance, there are always a good number of supporters and other key people in and around that person who made a significant but less well-advertised contribution. The self-appointed leader and spokesperson may have had the good idea. But most likely many others have bought into their vision and helped it on its way. And if it's going to be sustainable in the longer term, doubtless many more will have to join in as well.

I often talk about the distance leadership that is required to make Paradise Rescued work as a team and organisation. Without the trust, communication, local leadership and quiet conscientious management at our Cardan, Bordeaux winery in France, nothing would have happened. Whilst our French team prefer not to be in the limelight and media, that doesn't mean that their contribution is any less valuable. They bought into the Vision with its creator and jointly are bringing it steadily to life.

If you want the Vision to come alive, you have to make it happen. Drawing the picture is just the first step but not enough if you are seeking to create something special. Deploying the Vision as a policy or organisational strategy is something else.

Words on Walls are Worthless

If you visit a number of organisations, they will certainly tell you that they have a Vision of their future. They may even attempt to describe to you what they think it looks like. Quite often if you speak to multiple people at some organisations, you get a different interpretation of the same Vision. How does that drive a team forward to a common goal?

In other organisations, I see a different approach. I was recently visiting a highly successful and respected real estate agent in Melbourne who – to be fair – had done a very professional piece of work for me. When arriving at the reception and having confirmed my appointment and host, I noticed a very well-presented Vision statement on the wall behind the reception desk. I asked the person at the desk if I might have a better look at their Vision statement. From the blank non-verbal look I received back from the other side of the desk, I knew instantly just how deep that Vision was (not) integrated into that team and organisation.

I asked again pointing to the ornate document on the wall behind the desk. "Oh that?" came the response this time. "Oh yes, I think so. Here!". The framed glass scripted gold on black item was then passed across to me.

Doubtless a fair amount of work had gone into its preparation but its leadership deployment – the how it was being used and put to work successfully in that organisation – had not even been thought about. A nice statement had been drafted by someone, presumably high up in the company, and posted on the reception wall. The person who would have most most familiar with it would have been the cleaner who removed the dust on a regular basis! There was no other evidence of their Vision in the two conference meeting rooms that I sat in.

I sometimes see less well-presented documents – simple typed up on paper and photocopied – around offices or work spaces. They look tired and under loved. They kind of sit there on walls and notice boards because everyone thinks that's where they should live. But are they actually doing anything useful?

Invariably, these written documents achieve very little. The telephone list or football fixture list next to them has much greater individual emotional impact. At the end of the previous chapter, I talked about making your (picture)Vision document "live", in other words ensuring that it is regularly reviewed for currency and updated. Your (picture)Vision must be live but you also have to *bring it to life*! Words on a piece of paper pinned to a wall do not achieve that goal. One of your greatest assets is wasted.

Get your (picture)Vision out there

As we discussed earlier, Visions can be confidential to the world outside of that organisation. And that's very reasonable. But if no one on the inside knows where they are going, how do you know which way to follow?

On the inside of an organisation, the Vision must be public, in order that the overall team can collaborate together to make it reality. As I stated previously – "If you don't know where you are going, you will end up where you are currently headed."

Your (picture)Vision must have a deployment policy or strategic use in your organisation. It has to be part of the business / operational model and integrated with the communication strategy internally. And externally, if you so decide.

And this is where the **RSA secret really kicks in**. Big time!

I have gone into a lot of detail in this book to highlight the advantages of a visual approach. Producing a (picture)Vision probably requires more effort, strategic thinking, internal discussion and team work to make it happen. Whilst probably taking longer to produce than a typed-up document Vision on the wall, the investment through deep thought and reflection is immensely powerful. It creates new options, innovation and pulls the organisation to a new common level of understanding. But if – and only if – the (picture)Vision is effectively deployed and communicated back into your organisation.

As highlighted earlier, studies show that when done properly, a (picture)Vision brings way more internal strength and motivational power to an organisation. A (picture)Vision is much more impactful that a few words on a piece of paper. Through our RSA, the picture goes to work with our minds day in day out, creating that focus in our minds. It's automatic. With a picture in front of us, viewed regularly, it will focus our minds on making that Vision come alive.

And the key to making it happen is to quite simply get the (picture)Vision out into the work place. The impact that a picture has on our brains through the RSA is significantly different to what a piece of paper with words can ever achieve.

Perhaps the best example of this impact is at our Paradise Rescued France winery. We are a small niche brand winery business. The main living room in the house doubles as the business office. On the inside westerly wall, close to the exit from that room into the kitchen and entrance hallway, we have hung three landscape orientated pictures. One picture is our

Mission – the view across the Cabernet Franc vineyard towards the 12th century church on the hill opposite. The second is our logo. The third is our (picture)Vision – the French version.

I can't tell you how often people – be they friends, visitors, suppliers and our own team members – stop as they go through the door and look at the picture. And then share a comment about its impact so far or the future that we are creating. The pictures or images say it all. No printed document with words can ever achieve that same effect. And in the process of regularly looking at our (picture)Vision they are impacted through their own RAS.

Where to put your (picture)Vision?

Every work place, every team organisation, every family has a place where they post information. Why? Quite simply as means of communication. Most communications require reading and mental processing to obtain a clear picture of what they convey. A picture short cuts the process and every time you look at it again it gives your RAS a re-enforcement of that picture.

Make different size colour prints of your (picture)Vision and laminate them.

- Meeting and Conference room walls
- Visual Management and performance boards – part of your results display. Top level Business Management System document.
- Small stand-up desk copies.
- Rest rooms, operations rooms
- On the desks of senior leaders / managers facing outwards towards the office visitor.
- And if your (picture)Vision can be shared openly, then yes the reception lobby is a great location for advertising and communicating your future direction. Make sure though that you include the front desk team in the communication process – they can be your best asset. The first words they

share with your visitors can often determine that visitor's impression of the organisation.

Talk to it

The next most important part about deploying a (picture)Vision is for leaders (and the organisation thereafter) is to talk about it. To communicate it. And to lead it.

To some extent, the hardest part of the Vision process should now be behind you. You have created a great asset. It has immense power if you can use it well. You need to capitalise on it like any other asset and use it to its maximum capacity.

Because a (picture)Vision "goes to work" by itself with people who see it regularly, there is a tendency to just assume that it will do what it's supposed to do automatically, and it therefore requires no further effort other than posting it in the right people centric places and bingo it will all just happen. A manager's dream? But an unrealistic expectation for even an optimistic leader. Future reality has to be earned and created one day at a time by the actions of people.

One picture is simply not enough.

The process of implementing a (picture)Vision also requires thought, strategy, persistence and good communication. The leader needs to develop a continual process for reminding the organisation of its future direction. During presentations, meetings, line meetings, inductions and all communications, talk to and make mention of the Vision. Preferably talk to the Vision directly on your presentation screen or on the wall adjacent to where you are standing. Make sure that your (picture)Vision is posted in those places where your leaders talk.

By talking to – and therefore teaching about – the (picture) Vision, this not only re-enforces the pictures plus future goals into the audience but most importantly, it increases its power and passion within the RAS of the leader presenting it. The more frequently we look at that convincing picture of the future, the more we believe it and our brains go to work to make it into reality.

Use the power of your (picture)Vision. Talk to it. Continually.

The top level document

If you manage your organisation using a business management system or structure, you will have processes in place that regularly assess organisational and individual performance. This may be an annual or more frequent goal setting and review process.

This is a system I use a lot myself. The (picture)Vision is the perfect top level document. At the second level underneath are the annual targets for the organisation which leads to the setting-up of personal action plans and staff appraisal / assessments as well as functional / group / department targets. And the final third bottom document is the results record or performance dashboard as I like to call it, where the performance against key targets, metrics and indicators is recorded.

In a three page process, you have a very coherent visible management structure which starts with a clear picture of the future through the (picture)Vision working its way down into each section of the organisation. Recording the progress is done against clear visible metrics. This is a simple process that can duplicated deep down into large organisations or can act as a stand alone activity for a smaller team. I have used it and seen it work very well in both settings.

Lead and the magic will work for you

There is no silver bullet when it comes to leading, developing and growing organisations. They all involve people. Done well, creating and effectively communicating a clear view of the future is a powerful way to engage the people within that organisation. This helps set up a win-win situation where not only does that organisation grow but also the people within it grow. One can rarely win without the other, despite what we like to read in the media. It's either a partnership or it will end up with two groups going in a different direction which is unlikely to provide a successful outcome for both parties.

A (picture)Vision is a simple powerful clear way of setting a future reality. Creating a (picture)Vision is leadership in itself. Deploying the Vision and making it happen will take your personal leadership to the next level.

But (picture)Visions can be personal too. Next, I will show you how to put them to personal use and growth rather than for an organisation.

Additional resources to assist you in the creation and further development of your own (picture)Vision can be found at www.thevisionguy.com.au/trifectaresources

Part D

At a Personal Level

9

Personal Visions and Life Goals

More than just corporate

I have made a deliberate effort throughout this book to talk about organisations rather than companies. While I would agree that this book could (and most likely will) be described as a business book. Having worked for large multinational organisations for much of my life and applied what I have written here, I know that what I write here works. It can work in even the largest companies. As the founding director of Paradise Rescued, whose mission is very local and sustainability based around a small village, I have seen witnessed the power that applying the (picture)Vision concept can achieve.

I have also worked over many years on personal development and coaching my teams and people. We all have dreams and, in most cases, they are deep down and rarely spoken. We all want to be recognised for being good at something. It's human nature. It's part of what we are. I see a lot of people try to brush off the idea with a *"no, I am just happy going along with the flow"* but that usually comes after many years of unsuccessful effort and put downs from those around them that forces too many of us into a position of comfortable or learned helplessness.

It doesn't have to be that way. I believe that everyone has something special and unique to offer in life. The challenge is finding what that 'something special' is and persistently putting it to good use so that the appropriate recognition comes full circle in the fullness of time. To this end, a (picture)Vision is an amazing tool.

It is an amazing tool because it gets to work on you – the person who matters most to any one of us! By consistently placing a coherent picture of your future on your RAS incoming filter and lens, by looking at a (picture)Vision that you have created for yourself will progressively change your personal self-belief. And you will start to see opportunities that you never saw before because your RAS will be wired to pick it from all the data around you.

The biggest challenge and the largest opportunity *is* you! It's personal. In most cases we are only limited by the amount of belief we have in ourselves. Changing that inner self image is the hardest thing to do. Why? Quite simply because the picture we have painted – over a long period of time – on your RAS and in your mind is hard to alter. You create it over a long period of time through many experiences across many years. You tell yourself that you either can or cannot achieve something or be a particular way. And this is painted onto our RAS; it becomes our self-belief.

Inwardly, you become comfortable with your own picture. And the more you practice it, the more comfortable you become with it. Outwardly, you may wish to make a change, but inside you stick to what you see. This is why New Year's resolutions are completely useless. In a moment of excitement at a particular time driven by a lunar cycle you announce to the world that you will lose 10 kilos. At 4am the following day, you head off to the fridge for a dawn raid! Why? Quite simply, you have done nothing to change your picture of how you see yourself. As you dive head first into the fridge, you further reinforce the self image you have progressively built on your RAS.

The first and most important person you have to convince is yourself. And to do that you have to build a coherent believable picture of what you and your future looks like. And this is where a (picture)Vision comes in. You can create the future picture of you.

Better still, (almost) the only person you have to lead, convince and help believe is yourself. I know – easier said than done, right?

Don't abdicate your life

This is the toughest bit to write in this book. In the same way, companies and organisations start to believe that they cannot succeed nor take themselves to a higher level. Organisations or companies are merely groups of individual people. When one or some of those people no longer believe that they can succeed, the mental change spreads quickly until everyone believes the same. Which is why when organisations need to change, they first need to change their people – normally starting with the leader at the top.

If a football team isn't winning and doesn't believe that it can or will win, it (un)happily achieves its goal every week. With a new coach and a different outlook and picture in our minds, quite often the results change. Once the team is winning again, they go into every match with that mentality. Winning becomes the new norm and they self programme themselves to win. They see themselves winning!

As individuals, when things are not going the way that you want them, then you too need a new coach. Unfortunately, the coach you need to fire is yourself! They are your thoughts and pictures that have made up that self-image. Changing coach is not easy, is it? You have to go down the hallway to the bathroom and take a hard look in the mirror, followed by a very crucial conversation with the person in the glass. Then start to reset the image, the picture that you carry round of yourself.

Typically, that conversation is not an easy one. It requires a huge amount of honesty and tough talk on both sides of the glass. The tragedy more often than not is that people walk away from that self reflection and decide to compromise their future. Effectively they choose to abdicate their life and potential away when they could offer the world and ultimately themselves with much more. They can choose an upward spiral of self-actualisation and possible fulfillment or downward abject disappointment and ultimate disillusionment.

We often fail to appreciate that children's books and films contain many strong messages for adults. After all, they are written by adults, right? We usually see them as 'happy ever after' stories but miss the adult take-aways because it is just a children's story.

Revisit Disney's 1994 classic film *The Lion King* where the little good guy Simba grows up and comes back to retake his father's lion kingdom from the evil Uncle Scar. In the 'Remember who you are' scene, the self-exiled demotivated young lion Simba is led to the water hole by Rafiki where he initially only sees his reflection in the water. With some coaching from Rafiki, he begins to see the likeness of his father in the pond.

"You see, he lives in you" Rafiki explains as he ripples the surface of the water.

Simba's internal picture – the picture he has on his RAS – significantly shifts and his beliefs change about his situation and mission. The lens on his RAS is altered. He now starts to see a new picture. His vision shifts to what he might achieve and he heads back out of the wilderness to fulfill his purpose. And make his new vision into reality.

It's your life. And one of my greatest privileges (and

responsibilities) as a leader is helping and watching people make courageous decisions that ultimately bring about powerful positive changes.

Everyone has a voice

The follow on from the section above is about finding what each of us is good at, then making that our personal brand of excellence. We read a lot these days about creating "people of influence" coaching and training people working in a specific niche or area of excellence to grow their influence through a self-marketing programme. This kind of programme helps small business people to recognise their skills and knowledge have much more worth that they gave their credit for. They learn to bring their voice to life.

One of the greatest stories that fits nicely with the section title would have to be that of operatic singer Susan Boyle who went from ignominy to overnight success after performing *"I dreamed a dream"* from Les Misérables on Britain's Got Talent in 2009. She knew that she had a voice but had to find a way to get it out there. The results continue to be dramatic.

We can all only too often see wasted talent in other people. *"If only they could see it"* we exclaim as we look at those individuals, blissfully unaware that many people have said the same thing about them! Everyone has talent. You have a responsibility to yourself to work out what it is and put it to good use. For your own benefit, self-fulfillment and inner contentment.

I also find it interesting to read stories of those people who change their so-called 'career paths' in mid-stream. Our societal conditioning and images push us to some sort of career. At some point in that process – as Steven Covey talks in his audio work – *"we climb a ladder up the trees in the jungle to survey where we are going only to realise that we are in completely the wrong jungle"* and need to make a change. We normally self-justify our indecision to change on issues of family and money.

Find your voice. Create a (picture)Vision around what you and your future will look like. And yes....

Put it on the Fridge

The same principles apply for a personal (picture)Vision as apply to an organisational one.

Set about to prepare, think and then start drawing your (picture)Vision. The good news is that you are a committee of one and agreement with yourself should be an easy process. It is probably a great idea to get support and feedback from a real trusted friend who can be a source of encouragement as well as sharing tough-minded optimism. Going from the middle of the pack to leadership is and will never be a five minute game. That's why your personal (picture)Vision requires time to put together combined with strong balance about how much you can achieve in the time frame set. Be bold but not so "off the planet" unrealistically optimistic that you actually set yourself up for worse not better.

I advise caution in terms of who you seek out for help and support. It may be preferable to even find a professional coach who will give you honest and open feedback with genuine encouragement than ask a member of your family, who may try and hold you back from growing as it will show up their shortcomings which they do not wish to critically address.

As with all (picture)Visions they need to up and in and around where you are yourself in your home. They must be displayed somewhere where you will look at them regularly, ie more than once per day. Your home office is a good example and I suggest that you get a nice colour print out made and then framed or block mounted. Display it in a position when you have regular eye contact.

And yes you can put it on the fridge providing there is almost nothing else with it that may detract your RAS and mind from focusing on the picture. For instance, if it sits next to the monthly utility bill, its impact will be lost. It may also be that it will become dirty in that location and potentially be adversely commented on by other members of the household.

If the (picture)Vision is a family Vision, then the middle of the fridge door could be a good location for a laminated copy. In all cases, think about where such an important picture should be such that it has pride in that place commensurate with the level of importance that you want to attach to it. Consider making a postcard size print and framing it to stand on the bedside table. Your subconscious mind is your most powerful ally. Give it the picture through your RAS and let it go to work for you.

What you see is what you get

I want to close out this chapter reminding you of the core principle of (picture)Visions.

All individuals will have ups and downs courtesy of what life offers up by the way of challenges. Maintaining a strong healthy attitude is a learned process through which you learn how to respond to stimuli or things that haven't gone as well as you might expect. As I explored in *It's Not About the Dirt*, you can learn how to respond to those events and use them to empower you through your ability to respond in a measured way or you can react with emotion and follow through with personal put-downs or desire for recrimination.

The key question to ask yourself is *"What does it look like?"* In other words, what does your future look like? What do you want it to look like? Draw those thoughts as a picture using the techniques given in the earlier chapters of this book, deploy your picture to maximise the adoption of the picture into your mind and let it get to work.

I can't wait to hear your stories…

> *"Get a clear mental picture, fill it*
> *with emotion and drive on."*
>
> Skip Ross , Dynamic Living Seminar

10

Why Dreams don't Work but Visions do

Believing has to come before seeing

"I will believe that when I see it!" You may have heard that before and even have said it yourself occasionally?

People who make stuff happen, think differently. They have to because the world is so keen to put down and dismiss other people's ideas. As we develop a new idea, we start to build a picture of it on our RAS. This is turn feeds our ideas and creativity further to find solutions to bring it into reality. And the biggest enemy of a new idea in our minds is that undercurrent of disbelief or lack of supportive re-enforcement from anyone else which can instantly wipe that idea off our RAS.

At that point, a good idea can be lost. The power is with those power who – as in the case of Thomas Edison who 'failed forward' countless times to find a solution to create the light bulb – can continue to see the light despite all the dissuasion around them.

Our future and survival depend on our continual innovation. Our successful survival to this point as the human race has been on the back of all of our previous innovation. Every day and night, we create new and amazing brilliant ideas. The mind of a human being is dramatically powerful. Despite the fact that we lazily abdicate as much as possible to our digital tools around us. We think about countless new things every day but we either choose not to do anything with them or we do not know how to do anything with them.

If you were guaranteed success, how many more new things would you try out? In other words, if we could see it before we have to believe it, it would all be simple, right? You would just do it? You could just call up the desired outcome on your screen, there it would be and after pressing the ENTER button, we would be on the road to success! Bingo!

But life isn't quite like that is it? So, how do you believe before you see?

That's where the power of a (picture)Vision comes in. If we can capture (and develop with more thought) our future desired state as a picture, our RAS and our brain does believe that they can see the future outcome. And then they can focus and filter their effort to bring about its achievement.

Harness the power of our minds

When do you get your best ideas? Are you a morning person or do they come to you late in the day? What I encourage as a leader with my team members when they come up with a good idea is to 'hold that thought'. That is not to lose the idea, but to make a note somewhere and then let their mind get to work on it later. Why? Simply, because I know that in the busyness of our daily lives, one quick but important thought can get washed away by the next wave of new incoming seemingly urgent but incessant data hitting the RAS and the idea may be lost for ever.

We tend to assume that because we are not consciously deciding to sit down and think about something, that our brains are not at work or thinking. This clearly isn't true. For us to do anything, even the simplest of tasks or brain has to be working at some level or other. Remember about when you went to work or travelled somewhere today. Do you remember the car you were following or the person who sat next to you on the public transport? Clearly you were there, and your brain got you to your destination but some of the (less important) details don't appear to have been recorded?

Our brain is subconsciously working all the time – even when we are asleep. The ideas are being worked on all the time. The challenge is get them onto the front filter screen of your RAS so as they get priority over all the rest of the 'stuff'. If you can 'hold that thought' sufficiently strongly, your brain will eventually go to work on it and with enough self-encouragement or belief, come up with a solution.

Don't waste your Dreams – capture the ideas

I love his topic which is partly why I have held it back to the end. The creation of a (picture)Vision is a very powerful tool not only because of the result you achieve but also for the process of self-reflection and future examination that you do along the way that will help create a successful outcome.

Our culture yins and yangs somewhat over the use of the word 'dream'. Sometimes it is revered as in the case of Dr Martin Luther Kings' 'I have a Dream' speech in 1963. He was a very talented orator and his words helped create a different world.

Generally, we are dismissive of people who talk of their 'dream' ideas as unrealistic and without their feet being on the ground. *"You are dreaming, mate!"*, *"That's Pie in the Sky"* or *"It won't happen here!"* These reactions come from people whose many years of unsuccessful attempts to make new things happen have not succeeded. And they neither believe that change and improvement is possible, nor do they want someone else to achieve something that they were unable to make happen themselves. Hence, it's easier to dissuade someone else's good ideas through dismissive commentary and simple put-downs.

So, who is right and is there any truth in the middle of this psychological war of words?

Dreams and ideas are good. We need them. But we need to capture them. It's just what we do with them that needs a new approach. We need to be able to capture the great ideas and convert them into seriously good change and actions. In between those fleeting moments of inspiration, those dreams and a potentially exciting outcome, there is a gap that has to be bridged.

If we want to put those ideas to good use, we need to a plan to do that. There is always too much happening around us that gets in the way of making those big dreams happen. To ensure that we don't lose those ideas, we need to *convert them quickly* into pictures. Dreams don't work well because we never follow through on them. And so over time, through learned lack of success, we give up on them altogether. But if we can create a pathway to success through a (picture)Vision – a clear drawing of the future success – then we have made the first bridge to holding onto that dream and its chance of success will multiply rapidly as our RAS and brain get to work to make it happen.

"A man / woman with a Dream will not be denied."

Louie Carrillo.

Part E

An Ongoing
Success Story

11

Picture Visions
at Work

It may be a little easy to assume that as you read this book that once you have a (picture)Vision drawn and 'at work' in your life, business or organisation, that it will suddenly work like magic. As we talked earlier, we live in a 'give it to me faster and faster' world and we are all looking for that golden shortcut that make it all happen instantly while we sit on the beach to relax in the sun.

The main benefit of a (picture)Vision is that you have a roadmap and a clear picture of what the goal looks like. However, there is still no substitute for hard work and making it happen. Achievement is not automatic just because you drew a picture on a piece of paper and put it on your wall. There is no substitute for hard work, personal development and passion.

At Paradise Rescued, we have certainly needed plenty of those last three traits plus our (picture)Vision. But it certainly started with that clear picture Vision. It was our road map. Without it, the goal in our minds would have changed and with such a small team spread across the world, we would have changed directions continually as wave after wave of challenges came in. As it happened, we have weathered those storms and are now ascending the mountain of success resolutely step by step.

The Merlot Phoenix Project

The whole Paradise Rescued project has run back to front! From a personal perspective and initial motivation to take action, protecting the block of vineyard land between our family house and the old farmhouse to the west was the number one priority. As anyone who has sat on the kitchen terrace watching the sun slowly set on a summer's evening can testify, that is a very special place. With such a unique feel that has empowered me to want to protect it at all costs. When I am not there, I miss it and do everything I can to get back there at the earliest opportunity. It quite simply created the mission for Paradise Rescued and the passion that says *"Failure is not an option"*.

As I relate the story in my previous books *From Cabbage Patch to Cabernet Franc* and *It's Not About the Dirt,* the so called Hourcat Centre block of land ended up being the last piece of land that we were able to acquire in the puzzle. Even with my limited viticultural experience or knowledge, I could see that would be a good piece of vineyard land if managed and cared for well. It had great attributes with a gentle north to south slope providing good drainage and sun exposure. Its history showed a lot of love although for the last so many years preceding our acquisition it had been neglected and was in a state of abandonment when we signed the contract to purchase.

At that moment of purchase – driven by our Vision - we were ready to start the rescue and re-vitalisation plan that has taken the best part of eight years to implement. At that time, the vineyard block comprised some 55 year old Merlot vines and a greater part of similarly aged Semillon vines, which were well past recovery and would have to be dug up. The vineyard was almost completely overcome with weeds, obscuring light and air from the ground and base of the plants. The double branched/*double guyot* old vines were sometimes barely visible when walking between the rows.

The recovery plan began, working vine by vine, recovering every old vine by hand until the 1/10th hectare block was recognisable as a vineyard again. Seventeen months later, we harvested our first tiny Merlot crop – the 2012 vintage, which when blended with some of our precious Cabernet Franc created our first Merlot Cabernet Franc Bordeaux blend and launched a new legacy under the BlockTwo brand name. This tiny vineyard became our test area for our revised soil management programmes which are now applied across the full property. We quickly learned that good soil powers healthy vines that produce great fruit that makes wonderful wine.

The former Semillon block of dead vines was cleared, the soil turned and organically prepared, left fallow for two years and then replanted in 2014 with young Merlot vines with the tiny area behind the garage winery replanted in Cabernet Franc as a test of this soil compared to our original block. The young vines were nearly washed away in the heavy rains of July 2014, frozen rigid in their first heavy frosts of January 2015, survived the late April frosts in 2017 and endured the searing endless heat and humidity of 2018. Their first serious crop was hand cut in September 2018.

We had a clear plan driven by the values on our (picture)Vision:

- Quality and Excellence
- Continual Improvement and Innovation
- Sustainable Development
- Openness and Resilience

As well embracing our Tactical Plan by starting small, focusing on Quality not Quantity and learning through progressive experiment.

The Set Backs

We laugh now at the many challenges (learning opportunities) that came at us. Unforgettable was our disastrous loss in 2011 that I shared in *It's Not About the Dirt* and recalled earlier in this book. Our decision making during that crisis period was guided by what we had already set down in our Vision. We had a clear way forward even though the potential loss of a vintage threatened to stop us completely.

There have been numerous regulatory and bureaucratic changes, that have slowed our progress and threatened to emotionally throw us off the rails towards our goals. In the agriculture / viticulture business, every year is different and very often that difference is significant. Maybe all those differences occur in one season, as witnessed in 2018. Initial sales were slow as we fought to work out our sales / marketing portal, approach and strategy.

In short, 'stuff' happens! There will be challenges for all of us in life, with our goals and ambitions. And both as individuals or as part of any type of organization. If it really were as simple as just sending a letter to Santa Claus and then sitting back and watching it happen in a flash, then our value as a human being on this planet would be worthless. It's what we learn about ourselves and what we become in that process of achieving something very challenging that defines our destiny and our purpose for being here. Embrace the challenge and be happy that you are the one taking it head on to achieve something better for our sustainability.

The price and the prize

At Paradise Rescued, none of what we aspired to achieve was physically visible at the start. All we had was a mission, a dream that we had converted into a handmade (picture) Vision plus lots of passion and determination. Because of that amateur drawing, we pre-set our minds to lock onto the future image of our vineyard, winery and niche brand business. The title of my first book *From Cabbage Patch to Cabernet Franc* is no accident. We literally started with an exhausted over treated, grassless, sometimes flooded patch of dirt with a bunch of very unhappy vines. A real Cabbage Patch.

Our motto or tagline has become *"Failure is not an option"*. When you stand on the road leading to the winery and property and look to the west at the 12th century church, the answer is right there. As a tiny team, with our community and service providers around us, we have developed our own unique culture and passion. Compared to most other vineyard or winery operators locally, we go to extreme lengths to get things as close to perfect as we can.

And what kept us moving forward and believing that we could achieve better things was that (picture)Vision. We could see the future in our minds; we simply had to figure out how to achieve it. As we did so, we eliminated our own self doubt as a small team. We talked only about how we could make it happen, not if. The (picture)Vision was our catalyst – our guiding star, our beacon of belief.

You may not be surprised to hear that there are still parts of that (picture)Vision that are yet to be realised. The winery is a work in progress. Both vineyard blocks are always a challenge to continually improve their soil and vine health – that's how great wine is made! As I mentioned earlier, a (picture)Vision needs to be updated and current. The process of continual improvement, stretch and personal development must continue. Paradise Rescued is now deep into its second five year (picture)Vision. Minor changes and adjustments have been made and will be made again with the third Vision.

At the same time, the evidence of our progress is very visible. And we are incredibly proud – and humble – of what has been achieved.

First up and foremost, the vineyards are still rural agricultural spaces, the view to the church is still clear and the rural heritage of our village continues. That is pride and achievement in itself.

That is our Mission and it is being achieved. Our purpose is successful.

Our business has won two international Stevie business awards as both a new business and for our marketing plans. Our first ever wine, the almost unique 2010 Cloud9 100% Cabernet Franc – just one of maybe ten varietal Cabernet Franc's from the world's largest producing region of that grape variety, won a Bronze medal in its first wine show. And its tasting quality continues to improve after more than nine years after vintage. From the whole project, two books have been written with this one being number three plus the new "The Vision Guy" brand established.

And all because of one (well thought out) picture – a (picture) Vision.

"Even though it doesn't exist, I see it.
That's the power of a (picture)Vision."

David Stannard

12

Let's Get Visual

In bringing this book to a conclusion, I would really like to emphasise the use of visual management techniques wherever you can for positive future focused results. Pictures have such an enormous impact on our minds through our RAS such that, ignoring their impact on our day to day lives, families and business is an error. When used in a project, a compelling image has a significant impact in aligning our actions to meet the picture we have built of the future in our minds.

A clear well thought out (picture)Vision of what you foresee, when well displayed and communicated, creates a lot of power over our activity and recognition of opportunities. It is relatively easy to achieve, requiring focused thought and planning as well as considered deployment plus committed follow-up. It is infinitely more powerful that a printed dusty statement hanging unloved and forgotten on a wall in the boardroom. Or wherever.

The three-point principles of **Mission Vision Passion** are easy to apply providing you use all three together.

1. Understand why you are trying to do what you are doing. Why are you there? It's called a **Mission**.

2. Get a clear picture in your mind of what you want the future to look like. Make it into a (picture)Vision, post it clearly where you and your team work and let your RAS, your mind as well as those of your team, absorb it every day such that it will help you find the clues and ideas you need to convert it into reality. Eliminate your self-doubt – the more you can see it, the more easily attainable it becomes.

3. Work out 'the how' to make it happen. Apply **passion** every day.

Use all three. Persist. I look forward to helping you develop your (picture)Visions and then listening to your success stories.

I know you can do it. Go make it happen.

Let's get Visual.

Acknowledgements

A lot of life, learning, reflection and observation has gone into 'Let's Get Visual'. I am proud not only of the book and how it opens the door on the power behind our sense of sight and its impact on our own human psychology but also of the people and experiences that have effectively created the learning. Which, in turn, has helped shape successful futures everywhere.

Victor Caune, Founder and International Coordinator Best Practice Network, for 'seeing' the opportunity so early, his tireless encouragement, networking, marketing plus guidance in creating this book. Thank you also to the Leaders and State Directors of the Best Practice Network for their support and the opportunities to showcase this book and its potentially game changing contents.

Dixie Maria Carlton, master publishing coach and founder of Indi.e. Experts, for (yet again) taking on the role of book coach, leader, driver and marketer. Thank you for seeing in Paradise Rescued and myself, what we are yet unable to.

Tricia Wiles, Sweet Graphic Design, for her tireless and brilliant design work for this book and brand Paradise Rescued. You have created another gem in our book series and set the wine world alive with the potential of our brand.

In the book I talk a lot about 'Mission' – our why, my why. So much of that starts with our neighbours and community in the beautiful French village of Cardan, Bordeaux. Your endless support and that picture view across the Cabernet Franc vineyard towards the 12th century church is our 'why' – to sustain the heritage of our village.

To everyone who makes up Team Paradise Rescued, a global micro network of Passionate people working together with that Mission in pursuit of our Vision.

For my family, friends and colleagues for your support through many long days.

I am humbled that we have so many fans and customers around the world who encourage us forward and for whose ideas and innovation I am continually grateful. Thank you.

About David Stannard

David Stannard – aka The Vision Guy™ – is the Founder and Owner -Director of Paradise Rescued. Born and educated in England, qualifying as a Chemical Engineer from Birmingham University in 1980, David has had a successful leadership career in the petrochemical industry in the UK, Netherlands and Australia, covering more than 35 years.

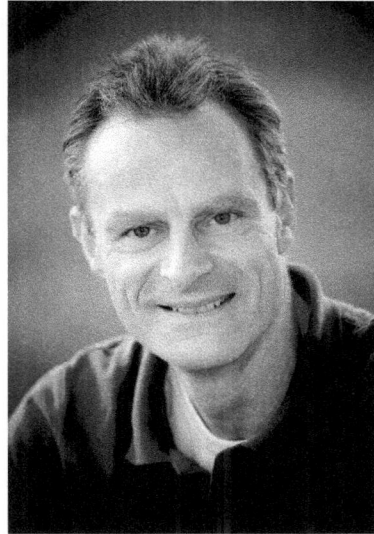

In 2010, as a tsunami of new housing threatened to wipe away the rural heritage of 'his' village of Cardan in the vineyards of Bordeaux France, Paradise Rescued was founded. David and his family had purchased a holiday home there many years earlier and wanted to preserve the tranquility of the area he'd grown to love so much. Working closely with the community, David successfully brought together a dedicated and passionate global team to manage the vineyard, winery, export marketing and business brand development.

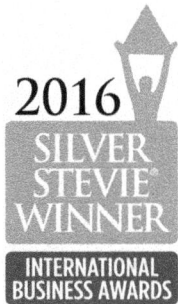

Today Paradise Rescued produces and exports organic red wines to Europe, Australia and the USA and is internationally recognised as a niche ultra premium micro wine brand. Paradise Rescued is a double Silver Stevie International Business Award winner - Best New Company 2013 and Small Budget Marketing Campaign (<$5M) 2016. The Paradise Rescued Cabernet Franc 2010 vintage was awarded a Bronze medal at the 2016 Melbourne International Wine Show. Using his insightful learning from many years of corporate leadership, David has used his experience to become The Vision Guy™, developing a simple but powerful model for personal and organisational success through the effective use of visual media and picture Visions.

Today The Vision Guy™, and members of Team Paradise Rescued are highly sought after as advisers and leadership partners for many international business projects.

Additional resources to assist you in the creation and further development of your own (picture)Vision can be found at www.thevisionguy.com.au/trifectaresources

To request more information on how you can work with David, or have him speak at your next event, please email david.stannard@TheVisionGuy.com.au

www.TheVisionGuy.com.au
Facebook.com/thevisionguy
Instagram.com/thevisionguy
www.linkedin.com/company/the-vision-guy

Other Books by David Stannard

From Cabbage Patch to Cabernet Franc

It's not about the Dirt

Essential Wine Tips